MW01002927

THE ART OF

BONSAI

Written by David Paget
Line art illustrations by Edward Baddeley

TOP THAT!™

Copyright © 2004 Top That! Publishing plc,
Top That! Publishing, 25031 W. Avenue Stanford, Suite #60, Valencia, CA 91355.
www.topthatpublishing.com

CONTENTS

INTRODUCTION

Bonsai means "tree in a tray" or "shallow pot." It also refers to the art of training and growing the trees. Many centuries ago the Chinese started creating miniature landscapes and trees, often using old trees from cliffs and mountains and transplanting them into shallow pots. The Japanese then started and eventually overtook the Chinese with their mastery of the art.

Bonsai trees in Japan are often passed from generation to generation and may be over 500 years old.

The Japanese have a special place in their house, which is an alcove or "Tokonoma." Here they display their most precious bonsai together with a scroll and an accent plant which may be a small grass or rock plant to complement the main tree.

In the western world bonsai is relatively new but becoming increasingly popular, and our skills are rapidly improving with these fascinating trees.

THE JAPANESE
SYMBOLS FOR BONSAI

You can get terrific inspiration by looking at the way trees grow in the wild or even in managed forest and woodland. Start to notice the trees all around you, especially in the winter when you can see, and appreciate, their amazing branch structure, and then try to emulate that yourself in miniature.

It is not only the branch structure and the effects of the wind or lightning strikes that will inspire, but also the exposed roots, or trees that have fallen over and re-grown. Sometimes a tree seed will germinate on a fallen tree and then grow over the rotting trunk. All of these things can inspire a scene to be created in a bonsai pot or on a piece of rock. You can therefore bring a piece of nature into your home, however small your yard may be.

If seeing a bonsai interests you, then don't be afraid to try it yourself. It is a combination of both horticultural and artistic skills and you may well have these skills without realizing it. Practice as much as possible and you will soon have your own collection of miniature trees that will improve over the years to come and provide you with hours of pleasure.

WHAT IS BONSAI?

Many people think that bonsai is a type of tree. This is not the case. You can turn hundreds of different trees and shrubs into a bonsai.

It is a way of bringing the beauty of nature into your house or yard. Bonsai were originally created as a way of bringing nature into the palaces of Chinese emperors.

You, too, can create a mature-looking tree or forest in miniature that looks and indeed might be hundreds of years old.

Depending on what style you choose, you can have a tree growing out of the side of a mountain, a forest, on the top of a hill or a single old pine standing on the horizon.

Bonsai trees are continuously changing as they grow, so are never finished. Unlike a painting or sculpture, bonsai is living art which you can alter and improve as time goes on. If you show them minimal attention over a period of time you may find that you have to re-style the tree by pruning and re-wiring to get it back to an acceptable form.

A bonsai, therefore, is a living art form that continually changes throughout the life of the tree.

Many people start with a Chinese elm because they are one of the easiest to keep and have small leaves. They can be treated as an indoor or an outdoor tree, provided you harden them off before putting them out in the cold.

Chinese elms (pictured right) are also very easy to use in any of the Japanese styles such as informal upright, forest group, cascade and so on.

7

Loropetalum

BUYING A BONSAI

When buying bonsai try to find a specialist nursery where the staff can give you all the help and advice you need for your tree to thrive. You can then feel confident that they are there in the future, should any problems arise.

If you buy from a general store, or in some cases by mail order, you will often find that there is no-one with experience on bonsai to give you advice and after-sales service.

When choosing a tree, ask what problems you may experience with that type of tree, what situation it prefers to be in, and find out about any specific problems such as different pests or disease.

Ask whether it will need re-potting in the near future and whether winter protection is required if it is an outdoor tree.

Don't be tempted to keep outdoor trees in the house unless you have several. Keep them outside most of the time and swap them around so that the tree in the house is only there for a couple of days at a time.

The best way to maintain their elegance is to do little and often with their general care and maintenance, therefore avoiding a major re-style.

Sometimes, however, you can suddenly see a way of improving the tree dramatically by cutting off a major branch, or changing the angle in the pot.

The twin-trunk dwarf blue spruce shown opposite is a fine example in the formal upright style.

SIZE OF BONSAI

There are four sizes of bonsai: miniature, small, medium and large. Miniatures go up to 2 inches (5 cm), small to 6 inches (15 cm) and medium to 12 inches (30 cm).

Bonsai up to 6 inches are called Mamé and ones between 6 and 12 inches are called Shohin, or one-handed bonsai (being able to be held in one hand). Larger trees are often known as two-handed or two-man trees.

Larger trees grown in the ground are often referred to as Japanese garden trees. This type of tree is quite unusual and is only mentioned to inform you of the full range of styles. They are not common and are less easy to tend.

The Japanese often style larger trees, using small ladders to prune them regularly.

The picture opposite shows a mature two-man tree (a large Chinese elm). The aerial root system is quite developed and is in excellent condition.

COMPOST & POTTING

Bonsai trees should always look in proportion with their pots, otherwise the whole artistic effect is ruined. Unlike normal garden or nursery potting, where the idea is to move into a bigger pot as the tree or shrub grows, with bonsai there should always be harmony between the tree and its pot.

Once the tree is styled it should go into a suitable pot for that size and style. If it is then to stay roughly that size and shape it could stay in that pot for life, but cannot stay in the same compost without having its roots trimmed.

Bonsai roots, as with other plants in pots, will grow round and round the edges of the pot and get longer and longer. What needs to be done from time to time is to remove the old compost to enable the roots to be trimmed.

The first thing to do is to take the tree out of the pot, comb the long roots down and then trim them back. The idea is to encourage new feeder roots near to the trunk of the tree.

Cut all long, thick roots back to the main root ball and trim about a third off the root ball itself, making sure it does not dry out in the process.

Use the compost dry, placing some in the pot first, then position the tree in the pot and push it down into the compost. This needs to be done before tying in. When you have checked that the position is correct you can pour in the compost all around the roots and use a wooden chopstick or something similar to poke compost gently between the roots. Do not make it all firm with your hands as you would with ordinary garden potting.

Some fine gauze is needed to cover the holes in the pot to stop the compost falling through.

If the tree is tall, top heavy or going straight outside, it should be tied into the pot. This is done simply by threading a piece of bonsai wire through both holes from the bottom and then twisting both ends together over the root ball to hold the tree firmly in place.

It is then necessary to re-pot, using a very open and gritty compost mixture. There are many different mixes you can use; try using equal parts of a proprietary, soil-based seed compost, $1/4$ inch (6 mm) grit and medium vermiculite. For some trees you can also use Japanese clay granules which retain the moisture but allow air and drainage between them.

14

You can then give the tree a good soaking with a fine rose watering can, if possible with rain water.

15

POTS & DISPLAYING

It is very important that you get the right pot for the right tree when it is good enough to display. Training pots tend to be deeper than the final pot to encourage growth. Plastic or mica pots can also be used but your final display pot will probably be ceramic.

There are many different shapes and colors to choose from and it is much easier if you take your tree with you when you go to buy the pot. Brown, unglazed pots are often used for evergreens such as conifers because they do not detract from the tree in winter when there is still foliage to look at.

A colored glaze is better for a deciduous tree. This gives some color in winter and can also provide a contrasting color in the summer.

Different styles require different pots; semi-cascade need a deep pot which keeps the branches off the ground, whereas cascade have taller pots but also need to go on a stand or overhang a pond, for example if the branches reach below the bottom of the pot.

Forest groups are often in shallow oval or rectangular pots but can go on a piece of slate or rock or even artificial rock.

To display your trees it is best to have a plain background to show off their silhouette. This could be the fence or your yard, or garage wall, or even a hedge, providing you can get behind your stand to trim it.

You need to bear in mind the position with regard to wind, shade, and so on, depending on which type of trees you have.

Thick-trunked trees go into a deeper pot and tall trees into a wider, shallower pot.

You could use monkey poles to display your trees. These are just single posts in the ground at different heights to suit your individual trees, with a piece of wood or slate fixed to the top of each post to stand your pots on.

Another way to display your trees is to use wooden shelves. Build them to suit your individual trees and add a small roof on the top to give some shade

from full sun, and shelter from heavy rain or sleet. You can then hang shade netting down the front in the winter to protect them from cold winds.

Reed matting or bamboo fencing also make a good backdrop for your trees. Another alternative is to place them alongside your greenhouse with the glass painted white and with shading material.

TOOLS OF THE TRADE

There are many different tools used for bonsai but you do not need them all at once. You can start with the basics, such as the ones included in this kit, and progress to more and better quality tools as you become more experienced.

To start with, you will need some small and large scissors for trimming small branches and roots; branch or side cutters to thin out main branches when creating a new tree; a rake or root hook for

re-potting; and wire cutters.
If you are digging trees out of your garden to style as bonsai then of course you will need a good shovel, a saw and loppers.

A sprayer for keeping roots or foliage moist is also necessary.

Coconut brush

Root hook *Rake*

Bench cutter

Metal scooper

As your bonsai skills develop, you may wish to accumulate a few more tools. There are various clamps and pliers for bending thick branches and soil sieves for taking out the fine material from your compost to improve drainage.

Metal scoops used for potting are very useful for pouring grit as well as potting compost into small areas. Brushes made of coconut fiber for cleaning or brushing off the bark or surface of the compost

are a useful addition to your bonsai tool kit.

A turntable can be useful when styling or trimming a tree so you can see it easily from different sides.

There are a whole range of power tools that can be used to carve out dead wood from the larger trees to simulate really old, partly dead and hollow trees, which looks particularly striking.

23

TECHNIQUES

When looking for a tree to turn into a bonsai, the first thing to identify is a good trunk and if possible a good set of surface roots. These are known as "Nebari."

The branch structure can be grown over a period of time. Some trees, however, will not produce buds where you want and it is therefore important in many cases to have some low branches.

The main technique for shaping a tree is to use bonsai wire (usually copper-coated aluminum) to hold the branches where required until they set in position, at which point the wire is removed.

The thicknesses of the wire required will depend on the width of the branch or stem.

If styling, for example, a beech seedling, you might start by twisting a spiral of wire, maybe $1/4$ inch (6 mm) thick, up the trunk so as to put some bends in it.

The branches may need thinning out to start to create the structure of the bonsai.

This will give the tree some visual movement. In this case it would be creating a style called informal upright.

A front needs to be chosen and branches placed on the left and right and also at the back to give better perspective. Keep the front fairly clear of branches so that you can see the main trunk.

The branches should not come from the same point on the trunk but should be staggered. Always place branches on the outside of the bend.

You may need to create some taper in the trunk for a realistic old-tree look.

A tapered trunk can be achieved by wiring up side branches as a new leader.

To get ideas for styling techniques, take a walk in local forest or woodland at different times of the year. You will get tremendous inspiration from seeing how trees form fascinating shapes with their branches and roots depending on the history of the tree. You can then try to recreate this in the styling of your bonsai.

Some trees are better shaped by pruning, or the cut-and-grow method, as it is also known. Some types of tree are too soft to wire but can be pruned to a bud to change the direction of the growth.

When wiring branches you must leave the wire long enough to go around two branches, around the trunk and along each of the pair of branches. This then locks them in place.

The step-by-step photographs below and on the following page show the correct way to wire branches, with thick and then thinner wire.

A twin-trunk style should have the division in the trunk as low as possible and should be placed in the pot with the thicker trunk to the fore to give better perspective.

This is also very important when planting a forest group. If the strongest and thickest trunks are at the front and the smaller, thin ones at the back, it gives the impression you are looking into a woodland with the far side appearing further away than it is.

A general rule is to aim for a triangle shape with the point uppermost. Another tip is to pull branches down because as trees get older their branches become heavier and therefore lower. By bringing the branches down you make the tree look much older.

Stand back and look at the tree regularly and use a plain background to help see the shape required.

PROPAGATION

Many bonsai are created from nursery stock or plants from gardens, hedgerows and the wild, but if you want to start right from the beginning you can.

Seed sowing is the way to propagate trees such as birch, oak, beech, chestnut, pine, larch or hornbeam. These are best sown in seed trays in seed-sowing compost or in the soil in a cold frame for a little protection. Most can be sown in the fall, when they drop from the

trees, but may take several months to germinate.

Cuttings are an easy method of propagation for many shrubs. Soft or semi-ripe cuttings can be taken from many varieties of plants, such as privet, lonicera nitida, conifers, escallonia, pyracantha and many more. These should be young shoots, about 2 inches (5 cm) long, taken in the summer and put in trays with plastic over the top to keep up the humidity. They will

These two relatively young trees show good shape and promise for the future.

need spraying with water each day until they have taken root.

Plants like privet and lonicera nitida can be propagated in the fall using thick branches as hardwood cuttings, which means you will produce a bonsai tree in quite a short period of time. Chinese elms can be rooted this way as well as semi-ripe cuttings in summer. Air layering and grafting are methods that can be used when more experienced.

THE BONSAI YEAR

Bonsai, when exposed to the elements, change color with the seasons. This is most strikingly apparent in the Japanese maple (or Acer).

During the winter when branches are bare you can see the structure of the branches and twigs. The Japanese prefer to show their deciduous trees in winter, believing the branch structure to be more beautiful than the leaf or blossom. In the spring comes the new growth and this is usually much brighter in color than later in the summer.

There is also fall color when the leaves stop growing and start to prepare to drop off.

Indoor trees, such as Chinese elm, do not change in this way with the seasons, but will slow development when the light levels are lower in the winter.

Acers in particular are fantastic in the spring with a wide range of colors, from reds and pinks to yellows and greens.

Many acers change in the summer to duller hues with some new color when they put on a second flush of growth.

Acers are well known for their brilliant colors in the fall but you also get fall color on lots of trees including larch, ginkgo, cryptomerias and many others.

Acer katsura in spring color

Figures and objects are sometimes placed around the base of bonsai trees, for various reasons. They can be to ward off bad spirits or purely for decoration. They can also give your tree an added feel of size and perspective.

BONSAI STYLES

There are many Japanese styles of bonsai. Illustrated over the next few pages are some of the more recognized styles.

Personal preference will dictate your choice, though all styles have their own individual beauty. The amount of space and time you are able to give to your bonsai may also affect which styles and specimens you choose.

Ginkgo bilobo

Dwarf lilac

FORMAL UPRIGHT

The formal upright style is not often used in bonsai. It consists of a perfectly straight, vertical trunk with branches precisely placed at right angles to both sides of the trunk.

This style is more difficult to achieve than an informal upright but if the right starter tree is found then it is well worth the effort.

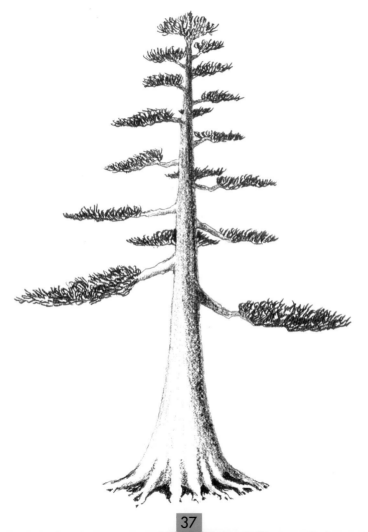

INFORMAL UPRIGHT

The informal upright has a curved trunk with the top finishing fairly central above the base. The left and right branches should alternate and, where possible, start on the outside of a bend. The main back branch gives perspective to the tree.

The curves in the trunk should be from side to side, not front to back, to enable you to see the flowing movement.

CASCADE

The cascade style gives the impression that the tree is growing out of a cliff.

The main trunk cascades down with foliage pads situated at various places from top to bottom. The trunk should bend when viewing from both the front and the side.

41

SEMI-CASCADE

The semi-cascade style is more horizontal than cascade but has the same effect of appearing to grow downwards from a cliff. These are often placed in a square, deep pot which is not as tall as a cascade pot.

ROOT OVER ROCK

This style comprises long exposed roots, which must clasp onto a rock before compost is added into the pot.

A deep pot or pipe will encourage the long roots to cling tightly to the rock to ensure that the finished tree will look realistic.

The top is gradually exposed to reveal the roots and rock, while the deep roots of the tree enable it to feed from the compost.

This style is not recommended for the beginner as a starter project, as it involves advanced techniques which the novice may find difficult.

45

The raft style refers to a single tree planted on its side with its branches treated as individual trees in a forest group. This is a useful style if you have a damaged tree, for example where there are only branches on one side.

In other cases you will need to cut the downward-pointing branches.

Removing small cubes of bark on the underside of the trunk will help to initiate roots all along the trunk.

The final result gives the appearance of a forest of individual trees but it is in fact branches joined on the surface of the soil by the original trunk.

WINDSWEPT

Unsurprisingly, the windswept style imitates a tree growing in an exposed place with almost constant wind from one direction.

The branches are still grown from all sides of the tree but are then forced by wires into one direction in horizontal lines. This gives the impression of a tree struggling against winds blowing permanently from one direction, much like the trees that can be seen on cliff tops, on prairies, or found on isolated, windswept beaches.

DRIFTWOOD

The driftwood style is meant to look like an ancient tree with lots of dead wood on it, as if it has suffered from lightning strikes and storms over hundreds of years.

This is achieved by using dead wood to its best effect in the design, or creating dead wood by peeling off some of the bark and using power tools or chisels to carve out the wood. If you do this, you must make sure you keep some veins of bark intact to supply sap to the living branches.

Another way of achieving a driftwood style is to attach a tree to a dead piece of wood in such a way that it looks like part of the original tree. This is known as the phoenix graft.

LITERATI

The literati style is usually tall and thin with very few branches, giving the impression of an old pine tree on the horizon.

Three branches are all that are needed, but the trunk shape and position of the branches are both very important for the style to work.

Literati is a very striking style and requires a good eye in order to achieve great results.

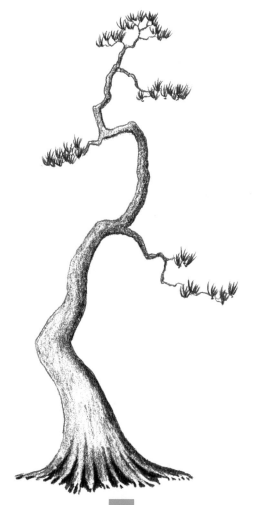

53

CLUMP

The clump style refers to several trunks coming from the same point at the base of a single tree. This is like a coppiced tree in woodland where you cut the tree off at ground level and encourage it to send up several shoots to regenerate growth.

This is a very pleasing style and gives the appearance of a mature and fully grown tree quite quickly.

FOREST GROUP

The forest group style refers to a miniature forest, usually with an odd number of the same type of tree.

The trees are roughly styled individually first, using different sizes of tree. The tallest and thickest trunk is placed at the front with thinner ones behind and shorter ones to the side.

The trees may be in two groups with a space between, and the individual trees should be placed with varying spaces between them.

The miniature forest is usually planted in a shallow oval or rectangular pot and the final branch placement arranged as one tree.

ROCK LANDSCAPE

This is a tree, or group of trees, planted on a rock which is then often stood in a shallow ceramic dish of water.

The tree roots have to be secured tightly with wire (KetoTsuchi), and sticky compost (Akadama) is used to hold the tree to the rock. Moss is used on the compost to disguise the root ball.

BROOM

The broom style is simply a short straight trunk with evenly balanced branches coming from the top. The effect is simple but effective, and when done well the tree can look very impressive.

This type is suitable for those new to the art of bonsai as it is reasonably easy to grow.

An ideal tree to start on if you want to create a broom-style bonsai is a Chinese elm.

SLANTING

The slanting style represents a tree that has been blown over at an angle so the branch structure has adjusted itself to the new position.

Alternatively, you may wish to think of it as a tree suffering from too much shade and stretching for light.

To create the slanting effect, the bonsai should be planted off-center in the pot.

BROADLEAF TREES

Obviously, the main care and maintenance tasks are watering and feeding. If this is done correctly then your trees will grow more quickly than you expect.

Regular trimming is vital in order to create the shape you want in your tree, and important when maintaining and improving the overall look of pre-trimmed specimens. New growth should be cut back with sharp scissors; this will keep it nicely twiggy.

It will also prevent the new growth shading out the original leaves and causing them to drop off.

Maples grow very quickly in the spring and can be pinched regularly, or left to grow a few inches to keep the spring color before cutting back later to the first pair of leaves. If you wish, you can leaf prune maples in June to reduce the leaf size. This must only be done on a healthy tree and no more than once a year. If you cut off every

In the fall clean up the dead leaves to discourage slugs and pests. Reduce watering to almost nothing in the winter.

leaf, leaving about half of each leaf stalk, the stalks will protect and feed the bud. As the bud develops the stalks will fall off and the result will be twice as many leaves, but they will be smaller and with fresh spring color again. It usually takes about three weeks to leaf up. This process also allows you to see if any branches within the tree need removing to improve the shape and structure. This would normally be done in the winter when the leaves are naturally off the tree.

General cleaning duties such as removing weeds and some mosses should also be done, and the pots, display area, and backdrop all kept clean. This all helps hugely with the appearance of your trees.

You may find that you need to turn them around occasionally to get light to the back of the trees, otherwise the back branches may become weak.

Some trees may need re-wiring to improve or change their shape. In early spring they may need re-potting, depending on when this was last done.

CONIFER TREES

Conifers are generally better when pinched out using fingers and thumb instead of scissors to keep the foliage in trim. If not you may get brown tips, which spoil the appearance of the tree. As a general rule, cut branches and twigs and pinch out the foliage.

Re-wiring may be required from time to time to keep the trees in the correct shape. Sometimes re-positioning a branch by a mere half-inch can make a tremendous difference to the tree's appearance.

Conifers like to be regularly sprayed over the top with water and also may need to be turned around to prevent weak back branches.

Watch out for red spider mites causing damage to spruce, and aphids damaging pines. Old needles need to be removed and new pine candles pinched back to keep the size of the tree under control.

Pines like to be in full sun all year round and kept quite evenly moist throughout the year. You may have

to shelter them from the rain in very wet winters.

Junipers may need finger pinching two or three times in the growing season to keep them compact and to keep the spaces open between the branches. Spaces in bonsai are as important as branches and need to be maintained.

Finger pinching is done to take out spines anywhere they are not needed on the tree, to promote growth in the right areas and to keep all the needles small and regular in size. It can be done with tweezers but that method lacks the "feel" of your own hands.

This is a fine specimen of conifer, which has had plenty of care and attention lavished on it, and the results are clear to see.

WATERING & FEEDING

Many people lose their first bonsai and it is usually because they do not realize just how often it needs watering.

Unlike normal house or patio plants, bonsai should have shallow pots. They should also have good drainage holes in the pots and feet to keep the bottom of the pot clear of the ground. All this, together with very open and free-draining compost, ensures that the small root ball does not become too wet,

causing it to rot. However, this also means it will require very frequent watering. It may even be needed more than once a day.

Feeding throughout the growing season is also necessary. Keeping bonsai small is definitely not achieved by lack of water or feed. You must keep the plant healthy to enable it to thrive. There are many different fertilizers but for indoor trees it is best to use a proprietary liquid bonsai feed about every two

When spraying, keep the nozzle about 2 feet (30 cm) away from the tree.

weeks in the spring, summer, and fall, and about once a month in the winter. Outdoor trees do not want any food in winter and can have the same liquid fertilizer as used for indoor trees at drier times of the year.

Normal garden fertilizers can be used but at a weaker strength than is recommended for ordinary plants. A lot of people are now using organic cakes which are made of rape seed and can be left on top of the pot, feeding the tree a little every time it is watered.

A watering can with a fine rose is fine to use outside. If you have a lot of trees you can use a hose but this will require a rose on the end.

Indoor trees could be put outside and watered with a can, or can be

placed in a bowl of water until the air bubbles stop. Then remove it and allow to drain. If you live in a hard water area and are able to collect rainwater, use this method to avoid getting unsightly limescale on the leaves and the pots.

The use of rainwater is best for both indoor and outdoor bonsai. Tap water is fine but in most cases it contains chemicals and salts which can build up in the soil.

Alternatively, storing tap water in a water butt outside for a few days will clean it.

Just as frequent watering is essential for the survival of your bonsai, drainage is just as important. Bonsai pots have holes in the base for this reason. If you are over-zealous with the watering can and there is no drainage, your root ball will rot and the tree will die.

PESTS

Bonsai get pests just like any other plant and they need to be looked out for so they can be dealt with appropriately.

Here are some of the most problematic pests you are likely to come across.

Red spider mite is the main pest for Chinese elm but it will feed on lots of other trees as well. They are extremely small and difficult to see. The symptoms are yellow, blotchy leaves falling off and fine cobwebs on the branches. Some pesticides do not kill this so check the label before buying. The spray doesn't normally kill the eggs and a further spray will be needed about a week later.

The red spider mite, shown here enlarged and in a small group about actual size.

Some bugs can appear with no warning and are best dealt with immediately. Use a similar technique to pinching out to catch the odd bug and dispose of it. One egg-laden bug could unlease a mini blight on your tree.

If you have a problem with any type of insects or aphids that seem rather persistent, seek professional help from a bonsai specialist. The trees are delicate and need just the right pesticides to do the job without harming the tree.

White fly is common on serissas and again can be killed using an appropriate pesticide.

Scale insects are particularly fond of ficus and acers. They are found on the stems but look like part of the tree. Treat with a spray or use fingers to rub them off.

Woodworm may not seem like an obvious problem but if you are developing a driftwood bonsai, you will have to keep a look out for telltale holes and treat accordingly.

Slugs and snails can also be a problem and are often found on the bottom of the pots during the day and up in the branches during the night.

Aphids of various colors can appear overnight, especially on Japanese maples, and need to be dealt with quickly.

Caterpillars can devastate some outdoor bonsai very quickly so watch out for them on silver birch and acers and generally, on all outdoor trees.

Vine weevil grubs in the compost are a problem, too, but you will not notice they are there unless you are re-potting or checking the roots because of poor growth. These can then be squashed or sprayed. See the picture, right, of an adult beetle.

If you see a vine weevil on your bonsai, dispatch immediately. If the weevil has laid its eggs, the danger remains in the soil and is hard to detect so be vigilant and check for pests at all times.

DISEASES

Diseases are not an enormous problem with bonsai but you do need to look out for them and try to avoid them in the first place.

Factors that make bonsai susceptible to disease are overfeeding, allowing the tree to dry out, and keeping unsuitable species indoors.

The three main keys to disease prevention are to ensure:

That the tree is well watered.

That the tree gets enough light.

That it is fed regularly and sufficiently.

You should also water the tree with some diluted fungicide when you re-pot and spray regularly with a fungicide.

If you are unfortunate enough to get a disease there are usually cures available.

Mildew appears regularly on hawthorn, field maples, oaks and crab apples and can be sprayed with a systemic fungicide as soon as you see white patches appearing on the leaves.

Rust is occasionally found on oaks etc. and the infested leaves should be removed and burned and, if necessary, an appropriate fungicide used to deter it.

Scab is most commonly found on fruit trees. Often the cause of the problem is that the bonsai has been fed with a fertilizer with too high a nitrogen count. If you notice a shrinking or drying area of bark, scab is the probable cause. As long as you have spotted the problem in time a spray from the nursery should provide an effective cure.

If you find a creamy white mould on the roots of a pine tree, this is **mycorrhiza,** which is a good thing as it has a symbiotic relationship with the roots, therefore resulting in a healthier tree.

When buying bonsai try to find a specialist nursery where the staff will be well informed and able to prescribe the correct medicine for your patient.

INDOOR BONSAI

Chinese elm is the variety most favored by beginners and can be kept as an indoor or outdoor tree.

They respond very well to pruning and wiring and are usually seen as informal upright, small broom style or root-over-rock. Occasionally you see them as cascade or semi-cascade but of course you can style in whichever method you prefer.

The main pest is red spider mite which is usually discovered when the leaves go yellow and blotchy and drop off. The tree will then need spraying with an appropriate pesticide and this treatment should be repeated about a week later.

Trim regularly to keep the shape and feed every two weeks in the growing season.

Chinese elm

The serissa root system, when developed like the example here, adds a great deal to the overall appearance of the tree, giving a feeling of great age and beauty.

The **fukien tea tree** is a small-leafed evergreen tree which has tiny white flowers turning to dark red berries. It can be kept in the house throughout the year but enjoys going outside on warm summer days. In the house it wants a bright position with not too much sun, as it can get overheated. Spraying the leaves with water and standing in a tray of wet gravel will be beneficial.

Jasmine Orange is evergreen with bright green pinnate leaves. The bark is smooth and light brown in color. Flowers appear at any time of year and are white with a sweet smell. The berries are red and look like tiny oranges. This tree likes plenty of light throughout the year.

Pistachio has lots of small evergreen pinnate leaves which are dark green and glossy. It may have occasional small green flowers.

Water regularly and spray the foliage. Keep in a bright position in the house and put them outside in the summer.

Serissa is also known as Tree of a Thousand Stars because of its many small white flowers. It will need trimming regularly but be careful not to cut off the tiny flower buds.

Japanese privet is similar to normal privet but needs a good sunny position and protection in the house in the winter.

Sagaretia is a tropical evergreen shrub with green leaves which are plum colored when first opening. The bark is flaky like a pine tree. It likes plenty of humidity.

Pomegranate is a semi-evergreen, depending upon how cool it gets in winter. It will either lose all its leaves until spring or just briefly in the fall and then re-grow. It has orange-red flowers and may set fruit.

Water it well in summer but sparingly in winter. Spray foliage with water in the summer.

It can be left in a bright, sunny spot in the house or placed outside in the sun during warm weather.

Jade (or money tree) is an evergreen succulent with thick, fleshy leaves and may flower with white or pink flowers in winter. This tree cannot be trained like a normal bonsai using wire but can be kept in a tree-like shape. It does not require a lot of moisture and if kept cool in the winter it will need hardly any water.

Paper flower is a climbing plant which will lose most of its leaves in winter if kept too cool.

The flowers are naturally very insignificant but what you may think are flowers are in fact very brightly colored modified leaves, or bracts. They come in purples, reds, whites etc.

They should be given plenty of water and the foliage sprayed throughout the flowering period. They need to be kept very dry during the winter dormant period.

Ficus can be grown from an ordinary house plant from the rubber plant family. This means that when you prune them they will bleed at first. Spraying wounds with water will help stop this.

They are often seen with aerial roots which start up in the branches and reach down for the moisture in the compost.

Olive is an evergreen with the upper side of the leaves a shiny dark green, and the underside gray and furry. It flowers in its native Mediterranean area with small greenish-white flowers before the fruit but may not flower in colder climates as a bonsai.

Keep a little drier in the pot than other bonsai but make sure you spray the foliage regularly.

It can be kept in a bright place in the house but will enjoy going out in the sunshine during the summer.

Sacred bamboo is generally evergreen but may lose its leaves if the temperature drops too low. The leaves vary in color from green to reds, oranges and mauve, changing through the seasons.

It flowers occasionally with small white flowers. It is very upright in habit and usually grows in a clump style.

Keep cool in winter but in a bright position in summer.

This podocarpus is a type of yew that is grown as an indoor bonsai. Grow near a window but not facing south. Prune anytime to keep the shape.

OUTDOOR BONSAI

Acer palmatum, otherwise known as Japanese maple, is a hardy deciduous tree well known for its spring and fall colors.

The popular acer palmatum has green leaves in summer and shows lots of orange color in spring just like the the acer deshojo leaf (pictured right).

Spring growth is very fast and it needs keeping in trim to prevent the shape from deteriorating.

Acer deshojo is probably the brightest red spring color of all the acers. It also turns green in the summer months.

Acer katsura is apricot yellow in spring and turns green in the summer.

Acer Kiyohime has a compact habit with green leaves. Sometimes leaves or branches need thinning out at the top to let air in—otherwise you may find you have problems with die-back.

Acer deshojo

Acer katsura

Acer kiyohime

Dwarf spruce

Dwarf spruce The picture shows a large specimen in training. Carving has been started and the tree has been wired and is still in a training pot.

Blue dwarf spruce This picture shows a recently styled twin-trunk blue form of picea albertiana conica which is approximately 3 feet (90 cm) high.

Blue dwarf spruce

Dwarf spruce forest. This picture shows the dwarf spruce but as a small forest group in a shallow oval pot.

Taxus cuspidata These yews are excellent for bonsai. They are evergreen and bud back into old wood very well. They also have small needles.

Taxus cuspidata—yew

Lonicera Baggesen's gold is a hedging type of honeysuckle with very small leaves which are evergreen and easy to grow. Cuttings will root as small or as large as you like.

Lonicera Baggesen's gold

103

Pinus mugo is a low-growing pine good for bonsai, especially for cascade or semi-cascade styles, as shown in the picture.

It is a good idea to fumigate the seed bed before planting as this will discourage pests and help prevent diseases.

Pinus mugo

Juniper blaauws needs finger pinching once styled to keep it in shape.

Juniper blaauws is one of the best junipers for bonsai. It actually grows upward but when turned down as a bonsai it works extremely well. The green foliage pads contrast well with the purplish brown bark.

Juniper blaauws

Escallonia have very small but beautiful rounded, serrated leaves and wonderful blue flowers. They are ideally suited for bonsai.

Japanese white pine can be grafted onto a black pine trunk for better bark qualities. Requires full sun and needs to be kept quite dry in the winter. Feed after needles have opened, otherwise they become too large.

Hinoki cypress A healthy specimen has very good, rich green foliage. It is slow growing and needs careful handling as the foliage is subject to falling off easily.

English elm is excellent for bonsai with small green leaves, which turn bright yellow in the fall. It can be used in all styles and grown from cuttings or suckers from the hedgerow.

Juniper pfitzeriana aurea is a common garden variety, expect training to last at least 4–5 years.

Keep it in shape by pruning with finger and thumb.

Juniper San José This juniper is widely used for bonsai and has both juvenile and adult foliage. The adult foliage is preferable and should be encouraged.

The bonsai pictured here is of the golden variety of juniper.

*An example of
Golden juniper.*

111

Ginkgo biloba This unusual tree is the only broad-leaved deciduous conifer. The leaves are green in summer and golden yellow in the fall.

Ginkgo biloba

Silver birch are very common and easy to find. They make excellent bonsai but take a long time to get a silver trunk when in a pot. If you root prune them and plant them back in the garden the trunk will thicken much more quickly and start to change color. You can then put them back in a bonsai pot and complete the styling.

Watch out for caterpillars that suddenly appear as they will strip its leaves.

The tree in the picture is in a natural raft style grown on a piece of slate. This was found in the woods and has a silver trunk laying down and a forest of branches coming from it.

Silver birch in a raft style

A field maple in training as a hollow broom-style tree.

Field maple is a common hedgerow tree which is easy to buy at nurseries and loses its leaves in the fall after turning an amazing buttercup yellow color.

They can be leaf pruned to keep the size down and grown in most of the normal Japanese styles.

Watch out for mildew and spray accordingly.

The small leaves and good color make the field maple an excellent choice for bonsai.

Field maple detail

Juniper blue star This picture
shows a tree dug from the garden
and styled into a cascade with some
dead wood showing.

Cork bark maple—most maples have smooth bark but this has very rough bark making it look older.

The **trident maple** is a
deciduous tree with green
leaves in summer, which turn
orange and red in the fall.
Roots can be damaged easily
by frost in a hard winter.

Trident maple

CONCLUSION

The aim of this book is to encourage people who may be interested in or fascinated by bonsai to attempt to create these amazing trees for themselves.

This is just a beginner's guide to get you started and there are many techniques that can be learned as you progress beyond the early stages.

It doesn't matter whether you are a child or a senior citizen, it is never too early or too late to start. In fact bonsai is particularly suited to the less mobile, as care and maintenance can be carried out indoors without any kneeling or bending over.

Bonsai societies exist in abundance and are a great forum to share your experiences. They can also offer help and tips to build up your skills, allowing you to show off your trees, perhaps in competitions or shows. The clubs often have guest speakers or demonstrators who will pass on their knowledge to help you to improve your own collection.

Many bonsai centers also run workshops regularly where you can have lessons in the art, and meet other people who have a passion for the hobby.

Clubs and workshops are often a social event as well as a learning exercise and you may find that bonsai can bring you a whole new way of life.

GLOSSARY

Accent plant	A small plant, often grasses or a herbaceous plant, used when displaying bonsai.
Akadama	Granules of Japanese clay used for growing bonsai.
Artificial	Home-made or false.
Bract	Modified leaf.
Ceramic	Baked clay pot.
Deciduous	Loses leaves in winter.
Feeder roots	Fine root hairs that absorb the moisture from the soil.
Flush	Spurt of growth.
Germination	Growth starting from seed.
Hues	Colors or shades of colors.

Humidity	Moisture in the air.
Mature	Old or aged.
Miniature	Anything on a small scale.
Phoenix graft	Attaching live material to dead wood.
Pinnate	Leaf made up of small leaflets.
Reed matting	Fencing made by wiring together individual reed stalks.
Seasons	Four times of year: spring, summer, fall, winter.
Silhouette	Outline against plain background.
Style	Form or shape.
Symbiotic relationship	Interdependent relationship of two organisms to their mutual benefit.
Systemic	Designed to be absorbed by the plant through its tissues.
Tokonoma	Alcove for displaying favorite bonsai.
Unglazed pot	Brown pot without a shiny finish, usually used for conifers.
Vermiculite	Exfoliated mica-like mineral.
Winter Protection	Some form of shelter from the extreme weather, i.e. greenhouse, windbreak material or other protective cover.

PLANT INDEX

Fukien tea tree	*Carmona microphylla*
Ginkgo biloba	*Ginkgo biloba*
Golden hinoki cypress	*Chamaecyparis obtusa nana lutea*
Golden juniper	*Juniperus x media pfitzeriana aurea*
Hinoki cypress	*Cham/paris obtusa nana gracilis*
Japanese privet	*Ligustrum japonicum*
Japanese white pine	*Pinus parviflora*
Juniper blaauws	*Juniperus blaauws*
Juniper blue star	*Juniperus squamata blue star*
Juniper horizontalis	*Juniperus horizontalis*
Japanese yew	*Taxus cuspidata*
Juniper San José	*Juniperus San José*
Larch	*Larix laricina*
Lonicera gold	*Lonicera nitida baggesen's gold*
Loropetalum	*Loropetalum*
Mountain pine	*Pinus mugo*
Needle juniper	*Juniperus communis repanda*
Olive	*Olea europaea*
Podocarpus	*Podocarpus*
Pomegranate	*Punica granatum*
Sacred bamboo	*Nandina domestica*
Sageretia	*Sageretia theezans*
Serissa	*Serissa foetida*
Silver birch	*Betula pendula*
Trident maple	*Acer buergerianum*

BONSAI